The Wild West in American History

COWBOYS

Written by Leonard J. Matthews
Illustrated by Andrew Howat and others

LIBRARY OF CONGRESS
Library of Congress Cataloging-in-Publication Data

Matthews, Leonard.
  Cowboys / by Leonard Matthews.
    p.   cm.—(The Wild West in American history)
  Summary: Describes the development of cattle ranches and the day-to-day life and work of the cowboy.
  ISBN 0-86625-363-7
  1. Cowboys—West (U.S.)—Juvenile literature. 2. Frontier and pioneer life—West (U.S.)—Juvenile literature. 3. West (U.S.)—Social life and customs—Juvenile literature. [1. Cowboys. 2. Ranch life. 3. West (U.S.)—Social life and customs.]
I. Title. II. Series.
F596.M334 1988
978—dc19   87-30699
                                         CIP
                                       AC

Britannica Home Library Service, Inc. offers a varied selection of bookcases. For details on ordering, please write:

Britannica Home Library Service, Inc.
310 South Michigan Avenue
Chicago, Illinois 60604
Attn: Customer Service

Rourke Publications, Inc.
Vero Beach, Florida 32964

COWBOYS

COWBOYS

Of all the heroes of the American past, perhaps none is as romantic or as exciting as the cowboy. He rode tall in the saddle and long in the stirrup. He knew right from wrong. He was quick to fight for justice and stuck to a friend come what may.

It is strange that the cowboy has come down to us only as an image. Wyatt Earp is thought of as the typical marshal, Jesse James as the most notorious bandit, and Custer as the best known Western soldier. There is no one cowboy, though, who stands out from the rest.

This is probably just as the cowboys would have wanted it.

They did not chase fame. The average cowboy was content to do his work well and draw his pay. Sometimes this work was tough and lonely; sometimes it was easy. On occasions it was dull and tedious, and every now and then it was nerve-racking. Whatever job he was doing, the cowboy was working with cattle and with horses.

Our image of the cowboy is of a man at one with his horse and his cattle. What is the real truth behind the image? What were cowboys really like? As with many subjects, the truth about the cowboy is even more interesting than the image.

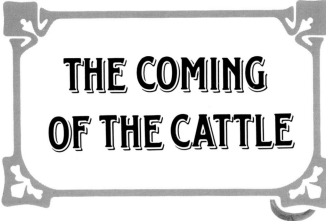

THE COMING OF THE CATTLE

Coronado and his intrepid followers marched north to Arizona with a herd of nearly 500 head of cattle.

Cattle are not native to North America. Before the white man came to North America, millions of buffalo and deer roamed the plains and forests, but there were no cattle.

The Spanish brought the first cattle to the plains, which were destined to become the greatest cattle range the world has ever seen. The very first of these animals arrived with Gregorio de Villalobos on the banks of the Panuco River in Mexico. The year was 1521. Soon hundreds of other cattle had arrived, and Mexico had a thriving beef industry.

As the Spanish conquistadores spread northward, they took their cattle with them. Francisco de Coronado marched north in 1540 with a herd of nearly 500 head. They traveled at least as far north as what is today the state of Arizona. Later explorers following Coronado found large numbers of wild cattle. These were the descendants of cattle turned loose by the early explorers.

Settlers continued to bring more cattle with them, until eventually Spanish cattle were grazing far into Texas. The Spanish settlers built up a very successful cattle industry in northern Mexico. They raised cattle for their hides and their meat.

Many of the objects later to be part of cowboy culture originated with the Spanish, who at this time ruled Mexico. It was the Spanish who first had ranchos, or cattle ranches. The high-pommelled cowboy saddle is copied from the saddles of conquistadores. The Spanish settlers also introduced the broad brimmed

The Texas cowboys could skillfully rope a longhorn steer at the gallop.

This is a genuine longhorn steer, menacing and dangerous as it prepares to charge. (*Photo: Denver Public Library. Western History Dept.*)

hat, which was ideal for conditions on the plains. High-heeled boots, needed to brace a cowboy in his saddle, and jangling spurs were also adopted from the Spanish. Chaps, worn on the legs to protect against sharp thorns, were a Spanish invention. Even the places where a cowboy worked, his ranch and corral, were patterned after those on the Spanish ranchos.

But the cowboy was not a totally Spanish creation. The way Texans borrowed Spanish ideas and changed them to fit their own needs created the true cowboy. For instance, the Spanish used a long pole called a desjarretadera. This had a large curved blade mounted at one end. It was used to hamstring cattle before slaughter. The Spanish also used long poles to place loops of rope over the heads of cattle. The Texas cowboy used the same rope, or lariat, but he learned to throw it with great skill. The cruel desjarretadera was no longer needed.

Perhaps the greatest contribution the Spanish brought to North America was the longhorn cow. This breed was ideal for the tough conditions in America. They were descended from the Andalusian cattle of the Arabs and were bred for life on the dry plains of Spain. The longhorns took to life in North America with relish. They were tough and strong enough to look after themselves on the bleak plains. Longhorns were big cattle with huge horns, which often reached six feet from tip to tip. They could fight off wolves and even pumas. All the longhorn needed to thrive was grass and water.

The disadvantage of these cattle was that they were half wild. Longhorns could not be pastured and handled like tamer breeds of cattle. They would unpredictably turn and attack a man with their fearsome horns. But the early cowboys did not have much choice. If a man wanted cattle that would survive on the plains, he had to have longhorns.

These were some of the legacies left behind by the Spanish. By the mid 1800s, the growing power of the United States had driven the Spanish out of Texas and the Southwest.

THE BONANZA IN BEEF

A noonday halt to water the cattle and horses. (Photo: Kansas State Historical Society. Topeka).

During the Civil War many Texans left their state to join in the fighting. Remaining on the land were thousands of cattle. When the fighting was over, the survivors went home to Texas. There they found that their cattle had run wild. Now there were millions of longhorns wandering around the grasslands of Texas.

Although the Texans had vast numbers of cattle, no one in the West wanted to buy them. These Texans were called cow-poor. They had a potential fortune but no money.

The big cities of the East, however, were eager to eat Texas beef. The solution to the Texans' problem was to drive their cattle to the Eastern cities. There were no cars or trucks at that time. The only way to move cattle from one place to another was to make them walk.

Of course, a cattle drive was not so simple. In 1866, when the first big herds set out, the country was still in turmoil. Several herds were attacked by outlaws. The cowboys were shot and their cattle stolen. In other places farmers stopped the cattle drives. The farmers were afraid that the Texas cattle were bringing disease with them. In fact, of the thousands of cattle that set out from Texas in 1866, very few reached a market.

Then Joseph McCoy came on the scene. McCoy, a cattle dealer from Chicago, had an idea. He believed that if a railroad could be built west into Kansas, the Texas cattle could be loaded on rail cars and taken East. After being turned down by several railroad companies, McCoy talked the Hannibal and St. Jo company into backing his idea.

McCoy chose the town of Abilene in Kansas as a destination. The town had plenty of good grass around it on which the cattle could graze. It was outside the reach of angry farmers. Most important of all, Abilene had a railroad. In the summer of 1867 McCoy started building stock pens and railroad sidings. He also sent a rider south to tell the Texas cattlemen what was happening in Abilene.

The first herd arrived before McCoy had even finished the pens. Soon thousands of cattle were congregating in Abilene. The huge herds of cattle could now be taken to market much more easily. This was the beginning of the boom in cattle that took place during the following twenty years.

Cattle ranching soon spread far and wide as cowboys drove herds onto any piece of land that had grass. In a few years, ranches sprang up all across the plains from the Rio Grande to beyond the Canadian border. The cowboy soon became the most important person on the plains.

THE COWBOY AND HIS HORSE

For twenty years the cowboy was the undisputed master of the plains. He rode, straightlegged in the saddle, across the long, empty miles. The great open spaces were his home. His way of life depended on his horse and his equipment, all of which was superbly adapted to the harsh conditions of the range.

The cow pony was descended from the horses brought to America by the Spanish. Some of these had run wild. Only the fittest and toughest survived a wild life on the plains. These eventually created the breed called mustang, the wild horse of the plains. These were the horses that were captured and broken to be cow ponies.

The ponies had a stubborn streak of independence, and there was no time for a long taming process. Cowboys tamed their mustangs by simply putting a saddle and a harness on them. The cowboy then mounted. The mustang at once tried to buck the man off. The cowboy just hung on until the horse gave up trying to dislodge the man. Many times the horse won the first round, flinging the cowboy into the dust. All the cowboy could do was climb back into the saddle and try again.

The expert horse breaker got to know all the tricks a mustang might try. There was the crow hop, the sun fish and the rainbow, all of them

Taming a wild mustang was a tough and dangerous job. Only top class riders could hope to survive.

bone-jarring leaps and twists made by the horse to throw the rider. This method of breaking horses was the origin of the exciting bucking bronco events at modern rodeos.

Once broken, the horse would be slowly trained in the skills of a cow pony. These skills were many and varied. A good cow pony was a highly prized possession. Though each cowboy might own his own horse, the working horses were provided by the ranch. Cowboys would ride different horses depending on which job they were going to do. Most ranches would have about six horses for each cowboy.

A newly broken horse would be used for the simple jobs that did not need much skill. These jobs would include riding line, or patrolling the more isolated parts of the ranch, and looking for strays. A horse that was a good swimmer was used when cattle had to be pushed across rivers. Longhorns did not like to swim. If they had horses to follow, they were more likely to cross quietly. Night horses were able to find their way in the dark without stumbling or treading in holes.

The most highly prized and most rigorously trained of all cow ponies were the roping and the cutting horses. Roping horses were used to catch individual cows, calves, or steers. Longhorns were dangerous animals and could easily kill a man on foot. The cowboy had to rope cattle from horseback. The roping horse was trained to respond to the slightest touch by the rider while he was busy with his rope. When the cowboy had roped a cow, he would wrap the rope swiftly around the saddle pommel. At this point the cow pony had to brace itself for the shock. The cow would usually try to break away. Only the strongest roping horse could hold a full grown longhorn when it wanted to escape.

Cutting horses were the most valuable of all the cow ponies. These animals were tough and agile. Cowboys used cutting horses when a particular cow had to be cut out, or separated, from her herd. The cowboy had to position his horse between a particular cow and the rest of the herd. The longhorn would try to get back to the herd. Whichever way the cow turned, the cowboy had to be there first to block the way back to the herd. Good cutting horses seemed to have an instinct for this work. They could turn around sharply and move from a standstill to a full gallop with a bound. It is little wonder that cowboys prized these horses so highly.

THE MAN AND HIS GEAR

The life of a cowboy was hard and tough. Very often his life depended on the equipment he carried on his horse. Everything a cowboy wore or used had to be practical and durable. The cowboy also had to

This photograph of an old-time cowboy illustrates clearly the typical Western saddle. (*Photo: D. Butcher Collection, Nebraska State Historical Society*).

be able to carry it all on his horse.

The saddle bore the weight of all this equipment. Though there were various styles of cowboy saddles, they all conformed to a set pattern. The saddles were built around a wooden frame. A strong iron core was fitted to the pommel to take the strain of roping cattle. The saddle around the pommel was often raised up to fit snugly around the rider. For the same reason, the cantle was raised high behind the seat of the saddle. This basic frame was covered by layers of tough leather. Cowboys found this shaped saddle useful in rough country or when working cattle. The shape helped the rider stay firmly in the saddle.

The saddle was held on the horse by two girths that were cinched, or tied, into place. This unusual arrangement was needed because roping a steer put tremendous strains on a saddle. No single girth or buckle could withstand the pressure.

Cowboys' boots had narrow toes to slip easily into stirrups and high heels which kept the spurs clear of the ground.

Spreading out from the saddle was the skirt, a square of leather, which gave the rider a better grip with his knees. Attached to the skirt were several leather thongs. These were used to tie objects to the saddle. These might be blanket rolls, yellow slickers (water-proofs), rifles, or a host of other equipment. To stay in his saddle, the cowboy depended on his stirrups. Cowboy stirrups were much larger than those used for other kinds of riding. The cowboy had to be able to leap in and out of the saddle quickly and easily.

All in all, a saddle might weigh over forty pounds. It was probably the only expensive thing most cowboys would own. A good saddle might cost a cowboy about four months' wages.

A cowboy's clothes were just as practical as his saddle. From head to toe the cowboy was dressed in clothes superbly fitted to his way of life.

The famous cowboy boots were a wholly American invention. The essential ingredients of narrow toes, high heels, and long legs only came together in 1878 when a cowboy persuaded a Texan boot maker to turn out a pair of

boots to order. The high heels served two purposes. They allowed the cowboy to brace himself in the stirrups. They also kept the large spurs attached to the back of the boots clear of the ground when the cowboy was walking.

Spurs were used both to help a rider hang on to a horse and to make the horse go faster. The reason for the large spurs was that the horses were small and the men rode with their legs straight. If the spurs had been smaller, a cowboy would have had difficulty reaching the horse's body. The large spurs also jingled pleasantly and cowboys sometimes wore fairly showy creations.

In the bitterly cold winters of the northern states, the cowboys needed chaps of goat's hair to keep them warm.

On his legs the cowboy often wore the most striking feature of his working clothes, chaps. Originally designed by the Mexicans as chaparejos, chaps protected a cowboy's legs in scrub and cactus. The Spanish word for a dense thicket of low, thorny shrubs is chaparro; in English chaparral means the same thing. The tough leather of the chaps prevented the thorns and prickles from tearing trousers and cutting legs.

In Arizona the chaps were famous for being huge and wide so that they protected the flanks of the horse almost as much as the legs of the rider. Elsewhere the chaps were narrower, almost hugging the legs. In the northern plains of Wyoming and Montana, a different style emerged. The cold winters that struck these states meant that the cowboys had to keep as warm as possible. They often covered the fronts of their chaps with goat hair. This gave them a shaggy look.

Essential to a cowboy's work were his gloves. So much of his time was spent working with ropes and reins that a cowboy's hands would have been rubbed raw within a few days. The gloves protected his hands. They were made of tough buckskin, but even so it was surprising how quickly a cowboy could wear them out.

The bandanna a cowboy wore wrapped around his neck was useful for many purposes. The cowboy could mop sweat from his eyes with his bandanna or tie up a wound. It protected the back of his neck from the hot sun and prevented possible sunstroke. He also wore it to cover his nose and mouth when winds whipped up the sand and dust. Despite this, many cowboys did not wear bandannas, and they were not as common as some people think.

The cowboy hat is perhaps the most famous item of Western clothing. When cattle ranching began cowboys were happy with almost anything that came to hand. The purpose of a hat was to protect the wearer from the weather. Soon, however, the scorching Texas sun caused the cowboys in that state to copy the wide-brimmed hats of the Mexicans. As usual, the Texans were not content with things as they were and improved the hat by giving it a high crown and a floppy brim. In the 1870s the round-crowned hat of hatter J.B. Stetson became increasingly popular. During the following decade the "Montana Pinch" style became popular on the northern plains.

The rifle and the handgun were tools of the trade for the cowboys who were hard workers, not hardened killers.

Cowboy hats may have changed over the years, but all cowboy hats have wide brims and high crowns. The wide brim is good for keeping both the sun and the rain away from the cowboy. During the cold winter months, the brim could be tied down to form a pair of ear muffs. The high crown was often used to hold water from which either man or horse could drink. The hats came in for a lot of hard wear. Cowboys have always been willing to pay a high price for a hat. A good one lasts for years.

Other items were of vital importance to a cowboy. Of these, the most famous are probably the rope and the gun.

The gun was essential to the cowboy, but he was not a hardened gunfighter as some movies suggest. In fact, the gun was a tool that a cowboy had to carry. He never knew when he might run into a puma or a wolf. Encounters with human enemies were much more rare.

A cowboy wore his gun when he was riding the range, particularly if he was near Indian Territory, simply because of the dangers he might encounter. He would also carry a gun when driving cattle. If the cattle stampeded, the cowboy might have to shoot a steer to save himself from being gored. On the other hand, when he was branding calves or working around the ranch, he did not need to wear a gun. Guns were heavy and could get in the way. At the same time, if a cowboy wanted to look his best he put on a gun. He might be taking a trip to town or calling on a lady. The gun was thought to be part of the proper dress for a cowboy.

The gun most often seen, of course, was the Colt revolver. Other makes were used by cowboys, but the Colt was the favorite. It weighed over two pounds, and its barrel was eight inches long. It was not a particularly good weapon for gunfights, nor was it very accurate. If a cowboy shot at anything further than 75 feet away, he was almost certain to miss. The Colt was designed for fast, effective shooting at close range. For this it was perfect.

For hunting or long-range shooting, cowboys used rifles. At the height of the cattle years, the most popular rifle was the Winchester. Most cowboys carried a rifle strapped to their saddles. These guns were certainly far more effective at long range than any pistol. Because they were much heavier and clumsier than a Colt, they were rarely used for close, fast shooting.

A cowboy's rope was essential for his work with cattle. Longhorns were famous for their bad tempers. A steer was likely to attack a man who came too close. The only way around this

Roundup time in the West.

A midday camp fire meal during the roundup. (*Photo: Wyoming State Archives and Historical Society*).

was to catch it with a rope and make sure that it was incapable of doing any harm.

The earliest ropes were made of rawhide and were about 35 feet long. Cowboys called these ropes lariats, from the Spanish words la reata, which mean "the rope." Rawhide lariats were easy to throw, but if a single string broke, the whole lariat was useless. In Texas, ropes made of maguey, a cactus-like plant, were popular. Maguey ropes were tough and threw well. They were often up to 75 feet long. They were of little use outside Texas, though, because they could not be used in wet weather.

The most popular lariat of all was made from hemp from the Philippines. These ropes were used throughout the West. They may not have thrown as well as rawhide or maguey lariats, but hemp ropes were strong and reliable in all kinds of weather.

THE YEAR ON THE RANCH

The most exciting and demanding time of year on any ranch was the spring roundup. This was the time when the cattle were brought in from the range to be counted and branded. After the long, cold months of winter, the cowboys could once again gallop across the plains. It was a welcome relief for the cowboys.

During the years immediately after the Civil War, roundups were still somewhat disorganized. They were called cow hunts, which describes them perfectly. The cowboys rode off onto the grasslands and into the scrub to hunt down any cattle they could find.

In the early days, many thousands of wild cattle roamed the plains. The first man to catch a steer or a cow and place his brand on it became the owner. An energetic cowboy could come back from a cow hunt as the proud owner of a sizable herd.

These unbranded cattle became known as mavericks. In 1847, Colonel Samuel Maverick acquired a herd of cattle in Texas. He decided not to brand them, since the cattle on all the neighboring ranches were branded. Unbranded cattle would be recognized as his, he reasoned. As the story is told, each time he heard of an unbranded cow or steer, he tried to claim it. The term maverick came to be used for any unbranded cattle.

By the mid-1870s most mavericks had been claimed. The old cow hunts turned into highly organized roundups. Every large ranch had a foreman and many cowboys, while a smaller ranch was run by the owner. He was also the only cowboy. Whatever their size, all ranches grazed their cattle on the open range. During the months of grazing, everyone's cattle mixed together.

Every year the longhorns had to be gathered together and divided up according to ownership. The new-born calves belonged to the same ranch as their mothers and needed to be marked with that brand. Branding was important because it defined ownership, and changing a brand was a serious crime.

At first, roundups were organized by the local ranchers. Later, they were controlled by local cattlemen's associations. A date and place were arranged for the start of the roundup. Cowboys from every ranch in the district arrived at the designated place. When the word was given, the roundup began.

The cowboys rode out in all directions looking for cattle. They might find some in small herds or alone. The cattle might be grazing or browsing in thickets. Wherever they were found, the cowboys would gather them together in small herds or bunches. Once gathered, the cattle would be driven back to the starting point.

While some cowboys were riding off in search of cattle, others built fires and started heating up the branding irons. They were ready to start branding as soon as the cowboys drove in cattle.

The herds were stopped some distance from the branding fires. Then the cowboys would start their rope work. The main task was to catch the calves for branding. The cowboys worked in pairs, one riding a cutting pony and the other a roping horse. The cutter would push his horse into the herd to separate a calf from the rest of the cattle. Once the cutter had

Cowboys often fought for their lives while protecting cattle from bands of outlaw rustlers and raiding Indians.

the calf away from the herd, the roper would move in.

Swinging his lariat, the roper chased and caught the calf. Ropers used different techniques to catch cattle. The "heeling catch" was used to drop the loop of the lariat just in front of the hind legs of a steer. When pulled tight, the rope tripped the animal and threw it to the ground. A "forefooting slip" caught an animal by its front legs, with a similar tripping effect.

Once the calf was roped, it was dragged to the branding fire. The roper would shout out the brand seen on the calf's mother. The branders would select the correct iron from the fire. Then they would brand the calf.

As well as branding all the calves, roundups served other purposes. One of the most important of these was cutting out the cattle to be sold. These cattle were usually about four years old. At this age the longhorns were fully grown, but their meat had not yet become too tough to eat. When all these cattle had been cut out from the main herd, they were herded together, ready to be taken to market. This

market might be many hundreds of miles away. Cowboys would have to drive the cattle for many weeks. The best and fittest cowboys were chosen for this task.

As the trail herds set off for market, the other cowboys returned to the ranch. These ranches came in many shapes and sizes. Some were plush, others were just a collection of sheds. Most ranches had the same problem: a lack of building materials. There were few trees on the plains, so there was little wood to build a house.

The early ranches were very simple. Some consisted of just a couple of dugouts. These buildings were nothing more than holes dug into the side of a hill. A roof was put over the hole and a door built at one end. Dugouts were dirty and leaked whenever it rained. But if a fire was built properly, a dugout was very warm in the winter.

Only slightly better than dugouts were sod houses. As their name suggests, sod houses were built out of sods of turf. These were cut from the prairie grass and shaped into large squares. The sods were piled on top of one another to form the walls of the house. The roof was built of wooden rafters, which were covered with even more sods.

In sheltered river valleys many more trees grew than on the open plains. Ranches located in the valleys usually had better buildings. The buildings had wooden walls and roofs, some even had wooden floors. Wooden buildings were bothered with fewer pests, such as rats and fleas. They were also easier to maintain. The best ranches were those with wooden buildings.

When cowboys returned to their ranches after the spring roundup, there were many different jobs for them to do during the summer. The job they liked least was called riding line. Each ranch had an area of land on which its cattle grazed. The ranch did not own this land, and several ranches might overlap. The ranches tried to keep their cattle on this area of land because it would make them easier to control. The cowboy riding line had to spend days on end riding along the imaginary line which marked the edge of the ranch's grazing land. He was expected to look for any strays that had wandered over the line. These he would drive back.

The line rider also had to keep an eye open for any tracks crossing into the ranch's area. These might mean trouble. In the early days of

cattle ranching, Indian raids were a very real threat. More than one cowboy was killed and his cattle stolen by Indians. Larger war parties might attack ranches, killing everybody they could find. Skirmishes between cowboys and Indians were fairly common. It was to deal with the Indians that the Texas Rangers were originally formed. In later years, with Indians confined to reservations, these raids ceased.

Most cowboys spent the summer riding around the range checking up on the cattle. If a cow or a steer was in trouble, the cowboy had to help it. One of the most difficult of these jobs was digging cattle out of bogs. Longhorns often stood in mud to find relief from the insects that buzzed around the plains. Sometimes a cow would become stuck in the mud. Cowboys had to haul her out with ropes. Once she was free, she was often so angry that she would then attack the cowboys who had just rescued her.

The insects also caused other problems. If a steer were injured somehow, a blowfly might lay its eggs in the wound. When the eggs hatched the worms fed on the steer, causing illness and even death. Whenever a cowboy saw an injured cow or steer, he had to rub ointment, often including carbolic acid, into the wound to kill the parasites.

Numerous other jobs also required attention during the summer. Cattle had to be kept away from locoweed and thick brush. Sick cattle had to be treated or isolated from the herd. The longhorns needed constant attention if they were to remain healthy.

Summer was also the time to catch, break, and train horses. Ranch hands would set off in large groups to catch wild mustangs. This was usually done by chasing the herd of wild horses into a prepared corral. Here they could be roped with ease. The initial breaking was often done by a cowboy particularly skilled at breaking horses. As soon as a horse would accept a saddle and rider, it was handed over to other cowboys to be trained.

The horses of a ranch were kept together in a

In the early days of the Far West, Texas was a lawless land and herds of cattle were often stolen by ruthless rustlers and Indian raiders. To combat this menace, the Texas Rangers were formed. They were tough men, able to ride all day from dawn to dusk during their hunt for wrongdoers. They wore no uniform but all knew how to handle a gun when the occasion arose.

group known as the remuda. Remuda de caballos is Spanish for "relay of horses." This remuda was looked after by a man called a wrangler.

Although the horses belonged to the ranch, each cowboy had his own string. This string numbered about six horses. It included horses skilled at cutting or roping and horses useful for their speed or endurance. Each day, the cowboys chose the horses from their string that they would need for the day's work.

Winter was the slow season for the cattle ranch. As bad weather approached, there was less and less work to do. Many cowboys were dismissed from the ranch during the winter because there was not enough work for them.

Those that remained worked at a variety of tasks. They spent many days inspecting and repairing their equipment. They wanted to make sure it would be ready for the next summer. Ranch buildings usually need repairs, and the cowboys also did this during the winter.

Occasionally, ranch hands needed to ride out to find the cattle. A herd might be stranded amid deep snow, while only a few miles away good grazing existed. The cowboys would drive the cattle to the fresh pasture. At other times, the cowboys would have to break the ice on ponds and streams so that the cattle could drink.

The cowboys who left the ranch spent winter in a variety of ways. During fair weather, they might hunt wolves. A bounty was paid on every wolf killed. A good hunter could earn a lot of money killing wolves. Other cowboys might drift into town looking for work.

Many cowboys, however, spent their time riding from ranch to ranch. Everybody knew they were out of work. The natural hospitality of the West was seen at its best in the winter. Any cowboy who turned up on a ranch was welcomed. The rancher and his hands were eager for news from neighboring ranches and the outside world. There might even be a few odd jobs for the drifter to do. The cowboy would stay for several days, with his food and lodging provided free. Then he would move on to the next ranch for a few days.

By the end of the winter, a drifter could find himself hundreds of miles from where he had started. As spring began to melt the snow, he would look for work on a new ranch. Most cowboys only worked at a ranch for a single season. By the next summer, they had moved on to another ranch.

THE LONG DRIVE

Driving the cattle to market was the most important job on any ranch. Without the money paid for the cattle, the ranch would fail and the cowboys lose their jobs. The trail drives were critical.

Once Joseph McCoy had established the practice of loading cattle onto railroad cars for the journey east, cattle drives became common. Ranchers all over the western plains drove their cattle to meet the railroad. Wherever cattle grazed, they were rounded up and driven to the railhead towns to be sold. The most important and impressive of these drives began in Texas.

After the spring roundups were completed, the prime four-year-old cattle were herded together for the drive. Sometimes a rancher would drive his cattle north himself. Other ranchers would employ a professional cattle trailer, or drover, to take over the herd.

The make-up of the herd was important. Fully grown cattle were the most profitable to drive, but they were the most difficult to keep together in an orderly mass. If a number of cows and their calves were included in the herd, the steers became easier to drive. Most herds were mixed in some way.

The size of the herds varied enormously. Small ranchers driving their own stock northward might only have about 500 head of cattle. The foremen of large ranches could have as many as 2,500 head. The drovers, who might be moving the longhorns of several ranches at once, could have even more. The average herd was between 2,000 and 3,000 head.

The herds set off after the spring roundup. At this time of year the fresh green grass was beginning to grow on the plains. The cattle had to be fed while they trekked north. Several hours each day would be spent grazing.

The need for as short a journey as possible

and the presence of good grass along the route meant that a number of trails were blazed. The most famous of these cattle trails was the Chisholm Trail. This route ran from the Red River Station, near the northern border of Texas, to the railroad at Abilene, Kansas.

Cattle came from all over Texas. Many herds had already covered hundreds of miles before they joined the Chisholm Trail for the 600-mile plod to Abilene. The trail was named after Jesse Chisholm, an early trader on the plains. He was the son of a Scottish father and a Cherokee Indian mother. He traced out the route from the Red River to Kansas just after the Civil War. Not too much later, hundreds of cowboys were trailing thousands of cattle along the route.

No matter where the herd started, the daily routines of the cowboys were very similar. Working as a cowboy on the trail was tough work. The typical outfit on the trail consisted of about a dozen men. The trail boss was in charge of the whole operation and was the highest-paid man on the team. There would also be a wrangler responsible for driving the remuda of horses. Each herd was driven by about ten cowboys. Some were young and inexperienced. Others were old hands who had trailed before. The cowboys were paid according to their experience. About $40 a month was the average wage for a trail hand.

Finally there was the cook. The cook was in charge of more than cooking. He drove the chuck wagon and was responsible for pitching and striking camp each night. He also had to check that the stores were in good condition and ration them. The chuck wagon was vital to the success of any herd. It contained all the equipment needed for pitching camp at the end of the day. It also contained food for the hands to eat during the long weeks on the trail. This was usually coffee, flour, beans, sugar, and bacon. When they needed beef on the trail they killed a cow.

With these simple ingredients and a few others, the cook produced what became staple

The average herd of cattle driven north amounted to between 2,000 and 3,000 head.

Western food. One typical example of this style of cooking was sourdough bread. Each chuck wagon carried a sourdough barrel. In this the cook put a mixture of flour, water, and sugar. This was then allowed to ferment naturally. After a few days some of this mixture was scooped out and mixed with more flour and water to form a dough. This was left to rise before being baked. The result was sourdough bread. Each day, more flour and water were added to replace the mixture that had been used. This way the fermentation could continue to provide a starting scoop for the next day's dough.

Because beef slaughtered on the trail was likely to be fairly tough, it was usually stewed. These stews were made with any ingredients that were at hand and were cooked for quite a long time. They were always tasty. Of course, huge steaks were favorite items, when they were available. Only a small part of a tough longhorn was tender enough to grill as a steak,

so such feasts were rare. If the cowboys were able to shoot any game along the trail, it found its way to the chuck wagon.

The cook was the man to begin the day on the trail. At dawn, he roused the men from their sleep with the cry of "grub pi-i-ile," and gathered them together for breakfast. After a quick meal of sourdough and coffee, the cowboys packed up their bed rolls and stored them on the chuck wagon. They saddled their horses and set out for the herd. The cook meanwhile tidied up the camp, and stowed everything on the wagon. Then he could move out after the herd.

The cowboys, meanwhile, would already have begun driving the cattle forward. Each day the cattle were expected to cover about twelve miles. This allowed plenty of time for grazing and watering. Whenever the herd reached a stretch of particularly fine grass, they would be allowed to stop and graze. Often the grazing would go on for some hours. All the

Trail bosses were often at a loss to understand the Indians' sign language.

time the cowboys would ride around the herd to make sure that no animal strayed too far from the trail. With the grazing complete, the cowboys would gather the herd together again. Then the long, slow march would continue.

The long trails from Texas passed through Indian Territory. This land belonged to the Indian tribes. Strictly speaking, the Texans should not have been there at all. But the cowboys had to get their cattle to the railroad. The Indians decided to take advantage of the situation.

They began charging the Texans a fee for the right to drive their cattle across Indian country. This usually amounted to a few cents for each longhorn. Sometimes, the Indians took their payment in the form of cattle. The cowboys had to cut out several head from the herd and hand them over to the Indians. Negotiating with the Indians presented a problem. Few cowboys spoke Indian languages.

One cowboy recounted how he once tried to talk to an Indian chief in sign language. This failed and so he tried Spanish. The Indian at once called forward two braves who spoke Spanish. They demanded ten cattle. The trail boss told the cowboy to offer two. The talking went on for many hours. The Indians seemed unconcerned about the time. Eventually the two parties agreed on a fee of four cattle. These cattle were paid to a small tribe. Larger and more powerful tribes demanded more.

Even after this toll had been paid, the Indians might return for more cattle. Sometimes young Indian braves would attack a herd and try to steal a few head for themselves. These swift raids, accompanied by war whoops and thundering hooves, were a serious problem to early drovers. From the 1870s on, the Indian attacks began to decrease. The cowboys, though, were always on the alert for them.

The large herds of cattle were worth a great deal of money, and drovers had to watch out for cattle rustlers. Large bands of rustlers would approach the herd and threaten to gun down the cowboys unless they handed over their cattle.

A favorite trick used by some rustlers was to pose as local ranchers who thought their cattle had joined the trail herd by accident. It was the custom to allow local ranchers to look for

their cattle. If they found a steer with their brand, they were allowed to take it. The rustlers, however, moved through the herd looking for any longhorn with a blurred or faint brand. They would claim such cattle as their own and drive them off.

It took a good trail boss to tell an honest rancher looking for lost cattle from a rustler. Even then, it might take some fast gunplay to drive the rustler away. The Texas Rangers were often found riding north of Texas in an effort to protect Texas cattle from rustlers.

Another obstacle that had to be overcome was the river crossing. Every herd had to cross several rivers on its way to market. There were no bridges on the plains in the cattle-driving days. Persuading longhorns to enter a river required a determined effort by the cowboys. If the sun was sparkling brightly on the water, the cattle would not take the plunge. If the river were flowing too quickly, the cattle would not enter. Sometimes, the longhorns would refuse to swim the river for what seemed no reason at all.

It could take hours of patient work to get the first cattle into the water. Once this was done, however, the rest of the herd would usually follow placidly. The cattle had to be kept moving during a river crossing. If the line of the herd became broken, the cowboys would have all the trouble of starting the cattle into the water again. Sometimes the cattle would panic in midstream and begin swimming around in circles. The cowboys then rode in among the cattle to direct and lead them to the far bank.

Other cattle might become stuck in mud or quicksand. The cowboys would have to rope these cattle and pull them out by brute force. One cowboy recorded that it took three whole days to get his herd across just one river.

When driving across open country, the herd took on a definite shape. Every cowboy had his job to do, and he knew it well.

At the front of the herd were the point riders.

The cowboys' gentle singing at night seemed to have a calming effect on the cattle.

These cowboys kept the lead cattle pointed in the right direction. Once this was done, the rest of the herd would follow in their steps. A little distance behind the point riders were the swing men. They helped turn the cattle, if the point men decided this had to be done. Otherwise the swing men joined the flankers in riding up and down the length of the herd. Their job was to keep the herd together in a narrow ribbon which could be controlled easily.

At the rear of the herd rode the drag men. The job of the drag men was to keep the stragglers from falling behind the herd. Riding drag was the most unpopular job on the trail. During hot days, the cattle kicked up so much dust that the drag riders almost choked and could barely see what they were doing. On wet days the hooves of the cattle kneaded the ground into a muddy mess. The drag men found themselves riding through a quagmire of mud. When the day's drive was over, the cowboys had to settle the cattle down for the night. The chuck wagon had been sent on ahead to the camping ground, and the cook was already preparing the evening meal. On a stretch of flat ground, the cowboys halted the cattle. Slowly, so as not to frighten them, they drove the cattle together. When the cattle were in a tightly bunched group, they were allowed to lie down. After being driven a dozen miles, the cattle were usually only too content to rest.

Even at night the cowboys had to attend the cattle. In fact night was often the most dangerous time of all. Taking turns riding the night watch, the cowboys grabbed what sleep they could. As one old-time cowboy remarked, "If you expect to follow the trail, you must learn to do your sleeping in the winter."

The cowboys on watch rode slowly around and through the herd. They always sang to the cattle. The sound of a human voice rising and falling in song seemed to soothe the cattle and allow them to rest. Longhorns were easily frightened. A strange figure suddenly appearing from the dark might startle them. If the longhorn heard the steady approach of a human voice it would not be frightened. The continuous singing of the cowboys was also a sign

to the cattle that all was well. The great fear of any cowboy was a stampede of frightened cattle at night. If cattle were nervous, a stampede could be started by the slightest noise. Humid, warm nights kept the cattle awake. If a thunderstorm then broke, the longhorns would get to their feet and start to mill around. The rest of the cowboys would be called out of camp. Some would ride through the herd singing their hearts out. Other cowboys would try to separate the cattle to stop them milling. Often the cattle would calm down.

Sometimes something would shock the cattle. Perhaps it would be a clap of thunder or a flash of lightning. It could be a carelessly dropped pan. Even the moon suddenly shining across the plains could start a stampede. In a split second the cattle would be charging off at a frightening speed. The herd would become a heaving, running mass.

One cowboy described the noise of a stampede as follows: "The sound of the rushing hoofs is imposing enough at any time, but heard mingled and confused in the running in the dark it is something terrible. A loud cracking of hoofs comes through the fog of sound, and the mad rattling of the great horns in the crush as the cattle struggle to head out of the suffocating press behind them and on all sides."

If the cattle were allowed to run unchecked, disaster would follow. Cattle would trip and be trampled to death by those following. Others would tumble down sheer drops to their deaths. The whole herd could be scattered across a hundred square miles of prairie. The cattle that survived and were found might be injured and exhausted by the run. It would take days to get the herd together again.

As soon as a stampede started, the cowboys were in their saddles and away. It was dangerous work. If a cowboy's horse stumbled and fell, the man would be pounded to death in an instant. A cowboy could race his horse over a

Cowboys who fell during a stampede were often trampled to death by the terrified steers.

bluff in the dark and die in a fall. Stampedes were the most feared of all events on the cattle drives.

The only way cowboys could stop the terrible rush was to leap on their horses and catch the leading cattle. If these leaders could be reached, the cowboys could turn them. By swinging the lead cattle around in a huge circle, the cowboys could make them join up with the rear of the herd. The cattle would then be stampeding in a large ring. Gradually they would calm down, and the stampede would stop.

Eventually, after weeks or even months on the trail, the herd reached the railroad. In the early years most herds went to Abilene. Towns such as Dodge City, Wichita, and Ellsworth later became the destinations of cattle drives. Here the cattle were sold and the cowboys given their wages.

Many tales are told of cowboys raising trouble as they celebrated their journey's end. In many cases this was true. After weeks of hard, punishing work the cowboys often rewarded themselves with drinking sprees. More often, though, a cowboy headed first for a barbershop. There the cowboy would have a shave and the first hot bath since the drive had started. Next in importance was a trip to a store. The clothes the cowboy had worn up the trail were by now ragged and torn. He needed a new set of clothes. Sometimes a new hat or pair of boots was bought as well. Only after all this had been done would the cowboy slip into a bar for a quiet drink and perhaps a game of cards.

Driving a herd of longhorns up the trail was long and tough work. The cowboy needed to relax when his work was all done.

THE END OF THE ERA

A rancher would order a sheepman to remove his flock from the range. Refusal might result in the death of the sheep and the sheepman as well.

For the twenty years after the Civil War, the cowboy owned the West. There were a few miners and even some farmers to be seen, but the cowboy was the most important and by far the most impressive figure on the western plains.

Suddenly the age of the cowboy was over. Although they continued their work, cowboys no longer dominated the West. They found themselves sharing the land with their rivals the sheepherders.

The cattle ranchers had arrived on the range first, and they believed that cattle were the rightful grazers on the plains. Furthermore, the cattle ranchers pointed out, sheep destroyed pasture. They ate the grass roots as well as the leaves. Once sheep had grazed an area it could be useless for years. The extent to which sheep actually ruined pasture is not clear. But it is true that sheep crop grass so close to the ground that cattle cannot graze there until the grass has grown longer.

If a man tried to graze sheep on a section of range, it would not be long before a group of cowboys came visiting. In no uncertain terms the cowboys would tell the sheepherder to leave. If the man refused, his sheep could be shot. He might even be killed himself.

The struggle between sheep and cattle ranchers came to a head in Arizona in 1887. The Tewksbury family and the Grahams had been bickering for years. Then an astounded

Graham cowboy saw the Tewksburys driving sheep into Pleasant Valley. For the next fifteen years the two families carried out an increasingly vicious vendetta. Men were gunned down mercilessly. Eventually, the entire Tewksbury and Graham families were wiped out.

In many ways these sheep wars were pointless. They were fought for control of range that was rapidly disappearing.

In 1874, Joseph Glidden, a farmer from Illinois, patented a new type of wire. It was strong, tough, and cheap. Armed with a ferocious array of spikes, it was called barbed wire.

The big ranchers were the first large-scale buyers of barbed wire. They realized that they could use it to stop cattle straying too far from the ranch. Their cattle would no longer become mixed with those of other ranches. Perhaps most important of all, by using barbed wire, the ranchers could keep various breeds of cattle separate. They could then breed their cattle more carefully. The tough longhorn no

longer had the range to himself. Newer and better breeds, such as the Hereford and the shorthorn, were brought in.

Barbed wire also brought trouble. Some ranchers fenced in land to which they had no right. They cut off other ranchers from land where their cattle had always grazed. Inevitably fences were cut. Fights broke out between fencers and cutters. Guns were drawn and men were killed either cutting or erecting fences.

Another use of barbed wire proved even worse for the cattle rancher. The small farmer began to use barbed wire to surround his land. Unlike ranchers fencing land which was not theirs, the farmers had law on their side.

According to the Homestead Act of 1862, any man who farmed 160 acres of unclaimed land could claim it for his own. By law, ranchers had no right to the land on which their cattle grazed. Any farmer could come and take it, and thousands of farmers did just that. Slowly but surely, much of the open range was disappearing beneath the plow.

That was the situation in the fall of 1886. That year the snows came early. Within a short time, the land was covered by snow so deep that the cattle could not find food. The ranchers had to use their precious stores of hay to keep their cattle alive. In January, warmer weather came to the plains. The emaciated cattle found some food.

Then a savage blizzard struck. For three days the blizzard raged. The driving snow buried cattle and covered the whole plains in a deep white blanket. No cowboy could leave his home without risking death. People could hear the painful cries of dying cattle. There was nothing anybody could do until the weather changed.

At long last, spring came to cattle country. Cowboys rode out to inspect the damage. They found many thousands of dead cattle. More than half the cattle were dead.

HOME ON THE RANGE

There are still cattle ranches in the West and cowboys to work on them. Many changes have come to the cowboy's way of life over the years, but many things remain the same. Although he may use a truck to ride the line, he still has to know how to ride and rope.

The cattle he ropes are very different from those caught in the Texas cow hunts of the 1860s. Few longhorns are left, and it is probably just as well. Longhorns were large, tough, and aggressive. They had to survive on the plains during the long years when they ran wild. Their aggressive streak and huge horns helped them fend off attacks from wolves and pumas. They had the strength to wander over the range, seeking better pastures and fresh water.

The cattle that have replaced the longhorns have none of these qualities. They do not need them. They no longer roam the open range. Instead they graze on broad pastures of grassland, fenced in and tightly controlled. The cowboys can carefully nurse their pasture. The cattle are only allowed to graze on the grass when it is in the peak of condition.

During the winter, hay and feed is distributed to the cattle. They do not need to travel long distances to search for their food. It is handed to them. In really severe weather, cattle may even be brought into shelter.

Today's cattle do not need to be as tough as the longhorns. This has enabled ranchers to start raising cattle that are easier to handle and give better meat. Herefords, Durhams, and Angus cattle all found their way onto the plains to replace the longhorns. Some large ranches even started breeding their own cattle. The King Ranch in Texas has raised a sturdy breed of cattle named Santa Gertrudis. These are a cross between Brahmas and shorthorns.

Also very different is the life of the average cowboy. He now lives in comfortable rooms. The flea-infested, damp dugouts are no more. With modern roads and automobiles, ranches are no longer isolated. Cowboys can watch television when off duty. They can climb into a truck and travel to town for the evening. A century ago such a journey might have taken several days.

There is a tendency for people who have never roped a calf to dress like a cowboy. Many people on

Cattle are still branded on the hip by today's cowboys. (Panhandle Plains Historical Museum).

the western plains sport Stetsons, high boots, and bandannas. But if you put these people alongside the real range riders, you can easily tell the difference. A real cowboy wears his clothes with an easy grace, as if they were made for him. In a way, they were.

On the other hand, many parts of a cowboy's life have stayed the same. He still performs hard physical work. He rises early in the morning to begin the day's work. Though he might get into a truck, or even a helicopter, the cowboy still has his horse. For working cattle on the grasslands there is still nothing better than a good cow horse.

When a cowboy has to drive cattle out of the bush or separate one steer from the herd, he does it in the same old fashioned way. On horseback, the cowboy will carefully position himself between the cow and the herd. When the cow is far enough away from the other cattle, the cowboy throws his lariat to drop over the cow's head. In many ways roping is easier today. Modern breeds of cattle have shorter horns than the old Texas longhorns. Getting a rope to fall over the horns is far less difficult than it used to be.

As in the great days of the cowboys, roping is most often done during the spring roundup. In the old days the main reason for a roundup was to separate the cattle belonging to each rancher from each other. Today, the open range does not exist and the cattle no longer become mixed together. Yet the spring roundup still is a strong feature of the cowboy's year.

When the cattle are gathered together, the work begins. The new calves are cut out. They are branded on the hip with the brand of the ranch. This is no longer done to stop them being mixed up with another herd. It is the traditional stamp of ownership.

These branding irons have changed remarkably little since the great days of the cowboy. The handle is a long iron rod, and at its end is the brand. This consists of a pattern of iron which will leave the mark of the brand pattern. The irons are heated in a fire until they are glowing red hot. The branding iron is then pressed firmly onto the hip of the young calf. The hair is burned away and the skin singed.

No hair ever grows on the singed skin. The brand mark remains on the steer for the rest of its life. If the animal is sold, the rancher erases the brand with a recognized counter brand. The buyer then adds his own brand. Some cattle may end their days with half a dozen different brands on their hides.

The traveler out West may still see cowboys chasing cattle across the prairie. Cowboys still live on ranches. But there are very few cowboys today compared to the numbers found a hundred years ago. The plains no longer belong exclusively to the cowboys. They have lost much of this land to sheep ranchers, farmers, and housing developments. The great herds and the long trails may be gone forever, but the cowboy lives on.

IN THE DAYS OF THE COWBOYS

1521	Cattle are brought to Mexico by the Spanish.
1775	Daniel Boone carves out the Wilderness Trail from North Carolina to Kentucky, opening new land for settlement.
1800	The Harrison Land Act allows private individuals to stake claims to lands in the western territories.
1808	Congress forbids the importation of more slaves.
1816	James Monroe is elected president.
1823	The Monroe Doctrine states that the Western Hemisphere is no longer open to European colonization.
1829	William Lloyd Garrison proposes the immediate end to slavery in his work Genius of Universal Emancipation.
1830	The Indian Removal Act forces all Indians living east of the Mississippi to give up their lands and move west.
1859	A large deposit of gold, called the Comstock Lode, is discovered in Nevada.
1862	Richard Gatling designs a revolving machine gun.
1862	Julia Ward Howe writes the "Battle Hymn of the Republic."
1862	The Homestead Act grants 160 acres of western land to anyone who will settle and cultivate it. Wide open spaces where cattle roam become fenced in farmland.
1864	Nevada becomes a state and Montana is organized as a territory.
1866	Cattle drives begin from Texas to Kansas/Nebraska and beyond. These ordeals are known as the "long drives."
1869	Wyoming is the first state to give women the right to vote.
1876	Alexander Graham Bell invents the telephone.
1877	The first black man graduates from West Point.
1880	Gold is discovered in Alaska.
1880	James A. Garfield is elected president.
1881	Garfield is assassinated and his vice-president, Chester Arthur succeeds him.
1892	The General Electric Company is formed.
1893	Henry Ford builds his first automobile.
1896	Motion pictures are invented.
1896	The Supreme Court legalizes segregation. The case of Plessy vs. Ferguson establishes a "separate but equal" doctrine.
1899	John Dewey puts forth his theories on education in The School and Society.
1900	William McKinley is elected president.
1901	McKinley is assassinated and succeeded by his vice-president, Theodore Roosevelt.
1929	The Rodeo Association of America is started.